Short Term Rental Secrets Revealed

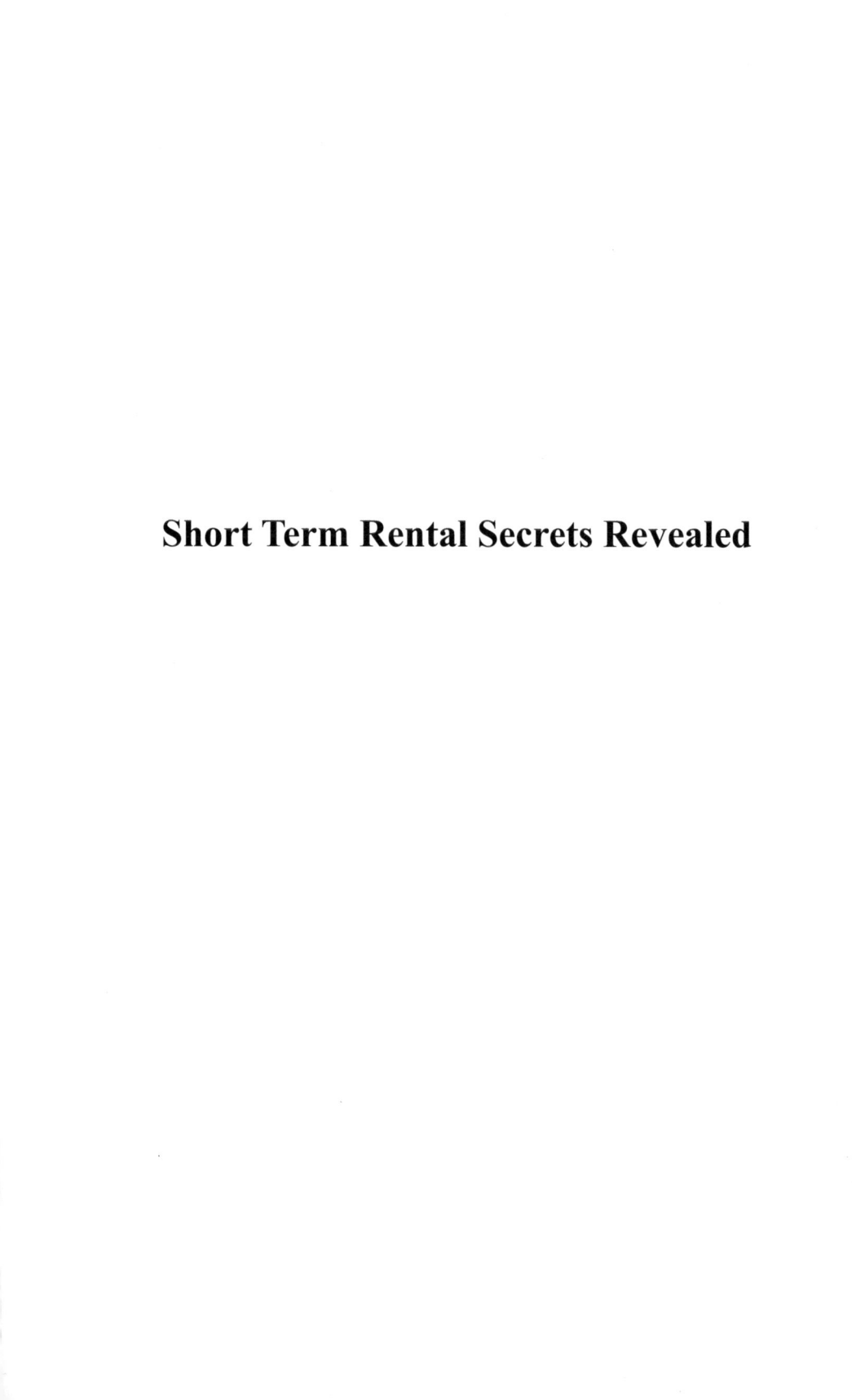

Copyright © 2024 by Norma Richards. All rights reserved.
No part of this publication may be reproduced, distributed, or transmitted in any form or by any means, including photocopying, recording, or other electronic or mechanical methods, without the prior written permission of the publisher, except in the case of brief quotations embodied in critical reviews and certain other noncommercial uses permitted by copyright law. For permission requests, email HappeeSpaces@gmail.com or write to the publisher, addressed "Attention: Permissions Coordinator," at the email address below:
HappeeSpaces@gmail.com

Ordering Information:
Quantity sales. Special discounts are available on quantity purchases by corporations, associations, and others. For details, contact the publisher at the address above.
Orders by U.S. trade bookstores, retailers, libraries, and wholesalers: Please contact HappeeSpaces@gmail.com or text request to 614-256-3470

Short-Term Rental Secrets Revealed / Norma Richards and Jerome Lewis
Amazon ISBN:

Typesetting and cover design by J.D. Williams
(www.behance.net/jdwilliams)
All rights reserved.

No part of this book may be reproduced, scanned or distributed in any printed or electronic form without permission. Please do not participate in or encourage piracy of copyrighted materials in violation of the author's rights.

Printed in The United States of America

Short Term Rental Secrets Revealed

9+ Things You Need To Know to achieve success with short-term rental real estate investing

by Norma Richards

Preface

The short/medium term rental business is a relatively new craze on the scale of a viable, popular and profitable business. Consequently, there are not many mentors available to help people that want to get into the STR business. So, I decided to address the top nine things I think are most important. Of course, there are lots of other details that can be addressed, but I picked out the top nine. This business is so dynamic, always changing and always new concerns, so it is definitely a process of learning. But I hope that this book will give you some insight, and an overview of how to get started. Just like my first book Free Ride to College: A Guide to Grooming Your Kids for Academic Scholarships; This book is a response to the many questions I encounter daily from curious potential investors. I am happy to offer classes for those who want more in depth information because there is certainly a lot more information that can be useful to make sure your business runs smoothly.

In addition, I have had lots of unique scenarios that can be addressed and how to handle them too numerous to name here. You can also check out the podcast and videos at **https://www.youtube.com/@JeromeLewis**.

Contact Us

Contact us directly
Email: **HappeeSpaces@gmail.com**
Website: **HappySpacesLLC.com**

Table of Contents

Dedication 15
Acknowledgments 17
Read This First 21
How To Use This Book 23
Free Gift For You 24
Foreword 25
Introduction 27
Secret 1: Make Your Exterior Appealing 29
Secret 2: Building Rapport with Guests 33
Secret 3: Ensuring Comfort and Safety 37
Secret 4: Live in Your Listing 41
Secret 5: Cleanliness and Scent of Your Listing 45
Secret 6: Build a List 49
Secret 7: Set Up Your Listing Like a Business 53
Secret 8: Independence from Third-Party Apps 57
Secret 9: The Importance of Building a Team 61
Secret 10: Conclusion 65
What To Do Next 68
About The Author: Norma Richards 71
About Happy Spaces LLC 77
Want Help Creating Setting Up Your Short-Term Rental? 78

Dedication

Jerome Richards, my husband, thank you for your everlasting support, I couldn't do what I do without you!

My children for always being my cheerleaders!

My siblings, friends and other family members for your encouragement.

You, the reader, for being someone willing to invest in your own personal and professional growth.

Acknowledgments

1. **Jerome R. Richards** - My husband for his constant support.

2. **Community of Real Estate Entrepreneurs aka COREE** - For connecting me with Jerome Lewis and other really smart real estate investors.

3. **Tancy Phillips** - My real estate agent who assists with properties when needed.

4. **The Real Estate Marketing Implementation Podcast by Jerome Lewis** - Because of Jerome Lewis and Norma meeting every month, this idea happened.

5. **Ohio Black Expo- Sheri Hamilton** -For helping to share the message of real estate investment opportunities with the community

6. **My team:**

Greenway Property Management- D.C.
www.greenwaycapitalproperties.com

JD Williams-Graphic & Web Design and Technology
www.behance.net/jdwilliams

Soledad Data Solutions.com
www.SoledadDataSolutions.com

The Sandwich Man
612 S. Yearling Whitehall, Ohio 43213
614-230-2501

Jerome Lewis -Marketing
www.JeromeLewis.com
Jerome Lewis(Real Estate Marketing Implementation) - YouTube

Golden Cleaning Services
www.goldencleaningpros.com

Dalton Cleaning Services
614-290-6453

Read This First

This book is an introduction to hosting and running a short/medium term rental business. I invite you to sign up for my class to get an in-depth, comprehensive scope of the necessary tasks, so you don't waste your time and money trying to figure it out. The truth is you should always supplement your business with your own marketing, website and systems to make your business independent of online platforms that can shut you down with no explanation. I know people that have had their entire business shut down because of third party platforms. Let me show you how to set up an independent business.

Visit the website and sign up to receive sign for more information:

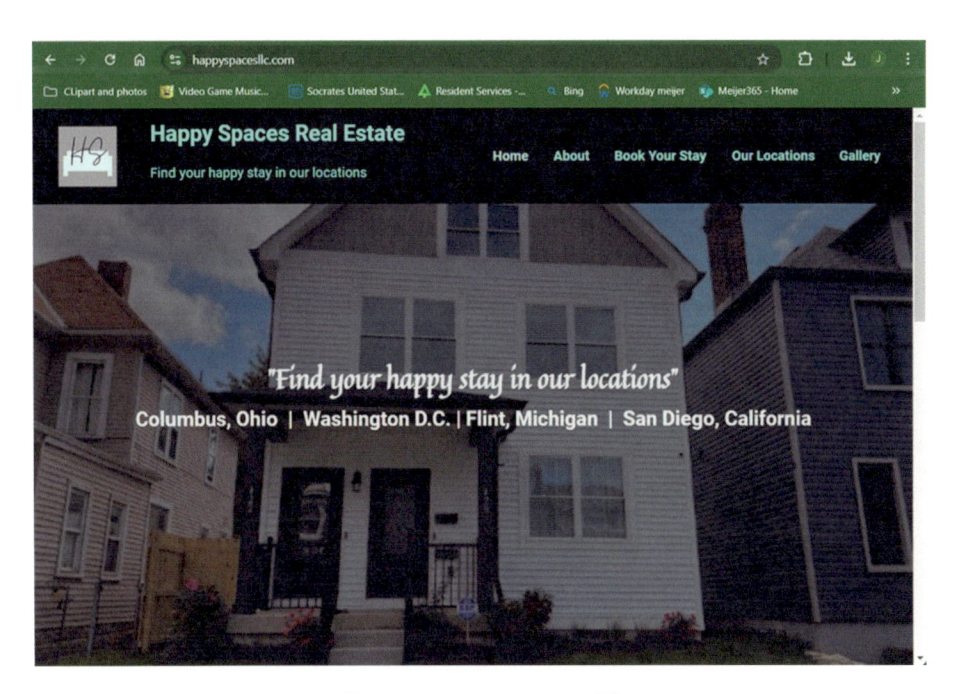

www.happyspacesllc.com

How To Use This Book

Welcome to Short-Term Rental Secrets, a book derived from a rich conversation between Norma Richards and Jerome Lewis. Originally conducted as a podcast interview, this discussion has been carefully transcribed and shaped into a readable format that shares Norma's invaluable insights into managing and hosting short-term rentals to build wealth in real estate.

Who is This Book For?

This book is designed for anyone interested in achieving financial freedom through real estate, particularly through the short-term rental market. Whether you're new to real estate or looking to expand your existing portfolio with short-term rentals, you'll find Norma's experiences and advice both enlightening and practical.

What You'll Find Inside

Inside, you'll discover a blend of practical tips and foundational concepts drawn from over 15 years of Norma's real estate experience. Here's how to make the most of it:

Read through each chapter to understand the core concepts and strategies Norma discusses; from making your property appealing, to mastering the independence from third-party rental platforms.

Focus on the key takeaways at the end of each chapter. These highlight the essential lessons and reminders that can guide your actions and decisions.

Implement the action items. Each chapter includes specific actions you can take to apply Norma's advice to your own rental strategy. These practical steps are designed to help you improve your operations and guest experiences immediately.

While this book aims to equip and empower you with valuable knowledge and actionable advice, it's important to remember that it cannot cover every aspect of the vast experience Norma has accumulated. For those who find themselves needing more personalized advice or specific help:

Reach out to Norma directly. At the beginning and end of this book, you'll find contact information where you can schedule a consultation with Norma. Norma is ready to offer professional assistance tailored to your unique situation in the real estate market.

Use this book as a guide and a starting point on your journey to real estate success. Dive into the chapters, take notes, apply what you learn, and don't hesitate to seek further guidance when you need it. Here's to building a thriving and profitable short-term rental business!

Free Gift For You

Jerome and Norma have a series of interviews that go into depth and talk about the topics in this book even further. To learn more, visit REmarketingPodcast.com and search "Norma Richards" to learn more.

There is also a Simple Short Term Rental Income and Expense Calculator available on Etsy to help keep track of your expenses and income for tax season.

Just copy and paste the link:
www.etsy.com/shop/HappySpacesCo

Foreword

It has been a rewarding experience to work alongside Norma Richards, in her various real estate endeavors. From the moment she purchased her first plot of land, she approached every project with a sense of purpose and determination. She went on to develop that land into a beautiful multifamily property, which Norma now manages as a successful mid-term rental. Being her real estate agent throughout this journey, I have had the privilege of witnessing her transformation from an aspiring investor to accomplished property manager and savvy business owner.

Norma's dedication to real estate investing and her willingness to embrace each new challenge with an open mind has set her apart in this field. Her journey is a testament to the power of perseverance and adaptability, qualities that are essential for anyone entering the world of short-term and mid-term rental investments. She has faced the same challenges many new investors encounter, from navigating zoning laws and regulations to handling the daily responsibilities of property management. Through these experiences, she has gained a wealth of knowledge that she now shares generously in her book.

Short-Term Rental Secrets Revealed: 9+ Things You Need to Know to Achieve Success with Short-Term Rental Real Estate Investing is more than just a guide; it's an insider's look into what it truly takes to thrive in this niche. Norma has meticulously documented the lessons she has learned, the strategies she has employed, and the pitfalls she has managed to avoid. Each chapter is filled with valuable insights and actionable advice that will empower readers to make informed decisions and build a successful rental business of their own.

What I appreciate most about this book is Norma's authenticity. She doesn't shy away from sharing her struggles, nor does she withhold the secrets of her success. Instead, she provides a transparent, honest account of her journey, making this book a relatable and practical resource for new investors. Her insights extend beyond the basics, covering everything from optimizing rental income to understanding market dynamics and managing guest expectations. Norma offers a realistic portrayal of what it takes to succeed, leaving no stone unturned.

Whether you are just beginning your investment journey or looking to expand your existing portfolio, this book will be an invaluable resource.

Norma's tips and real-life examples will guide you through each stage of the process, from initial planning to the daily tasks of managing a rental property. By the time you finish reading, you will have a better understanding of what it takes to succeed in short-term and mid-term rentals. Norma's story is an inspiring reminder that with dedication, the right knowledge, and a willingness to learn, anyone can achieve success in this industry.

Norma Richards has crafted a book that is not only informative but also inspiring. It is a must-read for any aspiring investor looking to make a mark in the rental market. As someone who has had the pleasure of working closely with Norma and witnessing her success firsthand, I can say with confidence that the insights in this book are not just theoretical—they are proven strategies that have helped Norma build a thriving rental business. I am thrilled to share this journey with you and to introduce you to the wisdom that Norma has gained along the way.

Tancy MASON-PHILLIPS, OPHP
REALTOR

"Your All-in-One Real Estate Expert – From First Homes to Commercial Ventures."

614-226-1014
tancy@tancymason.com
www.tancymason.com
960 N. Hamilton Road

Phillips, Administrative Staff

admin@tancymason.com

COLDWELL BANKER REALTY

Introduction: Secrets To Short-Term Real Estate Investing Success

Welcome to Short-Term Rental Secrets. In this book, Norma Richards, an experienced expert in short-term rentals, shares her top tips and secrets. Based on an engaging interview with Jerome Lewis, this guide is packed with everything you need to succeed in the competitive short-term rental market.

You'll explore ten key secrets Norma has used to excel in her career. Each chapter focuses on one secret, starting with making a great first impression with your property's exterior, and ending with how to run your rental like a savvy business. Here's a quick look at what each chapter covers:

1. **Secret 1: Make Your Exterior Appealing** - Learn why first impressions matter and how to make your property stand out to potential guests.

2. **Secret 2: Building Rapport with Guests** - Discover how to create strong relationships with your guests to improve their satisfaction and encourage them to come back.

3. **Secret 3: Ensuring Comfort and Safety** - Find out how to make your rental both comfortable and safe, so guests can fully enjoy their stay.

4. **Secret 4: Live in Your Listing** - See the benefits of staying in your own rental to understand and improve the guest experience.

5. **Secret 5: Cleanliness and Scent of Your Listing** - Learn the importance of keeping your rental clean and smelling fresh.

6. **Secret 6: Build a List** - Understand why you should keep a database of your guests to help with repeat business and tailored marketing.

7. **Secret 7: Set Up Your Listing Like a Business** - Get to know the best practices for managing your rentals professionally.

8. **Secret 8: Independence from Third-Party Apps** - Learn how to operate independently from online platforms to have full control over your rental.

9. **Secret 9: The Importance of Building a Team** - Realize the importance of having a good team to help manage all aspects of your rental properties.

10. **Secret 10: Conclusion** - Wrap up with a summary of all you've learned and tips on implementing these strategies into your business.

As you read through this guide," you'll find practical advice that you can start implementing right away. Whether you're just starting out or looking to improve your current operations, these insights will help you build a successful rental business.

Key Takeaways

1. Comprehensive Guidance: Short-Term Rental Secrets provides a detailed roadmap for success in the short-term rental industry, offering Norma Richards' expert advice based on her extensive experience. Each chapter focuses on a specific aspect of running a successful rental business.

2. Practical Strategies: The book is structured around ten crucial secrets that cover everything from enhancing the visual appeal of your property to professionalizing your business operations. This ensures you have a well-rounded understanding of both the operational and interpersonal elements necessary for success.

3. Accessible and Actionable: With a focus on practicality, this book is designed to be accessible to both newcomers and seasoned real estate investors. It encourages immediate implementation of the strategies discussed, helping readers to effectively apply Norma's insights to improve their rental business performance.

Action Item

- Before you dive into the next chapters, take a moment to look over how you currently manage your rental properties/business. Pick one area you can improve right away, whether it's updating the look of your property, how you interact with guests, or your marketing approach. This will help you use Norma's advice effectively and see immediate improvements in your rental business.
- With these straightforward tips and actionable advice, Short-Term Rental Secrets Revealed is your go-to guide to making the most of your rental property. Let's get started and unlock the full potential of your investment.

Secret 1: Make Your Exterior Appealing

Jerome: Norma, for our first Short-Term Rental secret, you emphasize the importance of making the exterior appearance appealing and ensuring the pictures are alluring. Can you explain what that involves?

Norma: Certainly, Jerome. The word "allure" means to attract or draw someone in. In the competitive world of short-term rentals, it's crucial that when potential guests see your listing, they feel compelled to stop and look. I focus a lot on making sure the exterior of my properties is eye-catching. For example, my husband takes charge of planting beautiful flowers around each property, which really helps in creating a welcoming vibe. We also choose paint colors carefully - modern and appealing, like a classic white with black trim, or even something with a bit of nostalgic charm, depending on the target audience.

How does enhancing the exterior translate into better guest satisfaction?

An appealing exterior sets the stage for what guests can expect inside. If the outside is well-kept and attractive, it suggests that the interior will be the same. This helps in creating a positive first impression, which is crucial in a market where guests often have numerous options.

Could you share some specific tips on how to make a property's exterior more appealing?

Absolutely. First, focus on landscaping—adding flowers or maintaining a neat garden can significantly enhance curb appeal. Next, consider the lighting. Good outdoor lighting makes the property safe and accessible at night, and can also enhance its beauty after dusk. Finally, choose exterior paint colors that are broadly appealing. Neutral colors like whites or soft grays tend to attract a wider audience by creating a clean and modern look.

And what about making the listing photos alluring?

Photos are your first opportunity to grab a potential guest's attention. Make sure your photos are accurate and show your property across different seasons. For instance, show your property's exterior with summer flowers in full bloom, or capture the cozy appeal during the winter snow. It's also effective to highlight any unique outdoor features like autumn leaves or spring blossoms to give guests a real feel for what to expect no matter when they book.

It sounds like a lot of thought goes into these first steps. Why is this so critical for a listing?

Jerome, in short-term rentals, you're not just marketing a space, but you are marketing an experience. The exterior and the photos are part of the narrative you're telling potential guests. A well-maintained and visually appealing property not only attracts guests but also reassures them that they are making a good choice. It's about making them feel they will be comfortable and secure, which is fundamental in hospitality.

Norma, thank you for these insights. It's clear that the exterior and the visual presentation of a property are as crucial as the interior amenities.

Key Takeaways

1. First Impressions Count: The first thing a guest sees is the outside of your rental. A well-maintained and attractive exterior makes a strong first impression and can significantly influence a guest's decision to book your property.

2. Details Matter: Small details like well-kept gardens, fresh paint, and good lighting not only make your property look good but also make it feel welcoming. Norma's focus on these details shows how important it is to consider what guests will first notice.

3. Setting Expectations: An appealing exterior sets the stage for what guests can expect inside. If the outside is well cared for, guests will anticipate that the interior will be equally pleasing, which starts their stay on a positive note.

Action Item

Research and Visualize: Before starting your short-term rental, spend time visiting potential properties or browsing real estate listings online. Pay close attention to the exteriors of these properties. Visualize the changes you might make to improve curb appeal, such as adding flowers, updating paint, or improving lighting. This exercise will help you understand what to look for and estimate potential costs, preparing you to make a well-informed decision when you choose your property.

Secret 2: Building Rapport with Guests

How do you build a rapport with your guests?

Building rapport is about creating a connection with your guests that goes beyond the basic host-guest relationship. It's crucial because it helps guests overlook small imperfections. For instance, if the wind knocks over a trash can or something minor goes wrong, guests who feel a connection with you are more understanding. I make it a point to call every guest before they arrive. This isn't just a courtesy call; it's an opportunity to understand their visit's purpose and to personalize their experience.

That sounds proactive. Can you give an example of how this has worked for you?

Absolutely. Just last night, I spoke with a guest who was visiting to see his brother's newborn. I learned he also had a four-year-old son with him. Knowing this, I suggested they visit the local firemen's museum, which is a hit with kids. This simple suggestion, based on understanding his situation, made the guest feel cared for and excited about their visit.

It seems like these personal touches make a big difference. Do you use a script for these calls, or do you keep the conversation more natural?

I start with a sort of mental script to keep the call structured. I greet them, welcome them, and then I ask what brings them to the area. This opens up the conversation. Based on their answers, I tailor the rest of the call, offering suggestions or additional help based on what they tell me. It's about making the conversation as helpful and personal as possible.

How do you maintain that rapport once they've arrived?

The day after they arrive, I reach out again to ask how they slept and if they have any questions or need anything. This follow-up is crucial; it shows that I'm attentive and care about their comfort. For example, this week a guest wanted local TV channels that weren't initially available. I figured out a solution with a new antenna and set it up for them, which they greatly appreciated.

It sounds like being attentive and responsive plays a big role in building and maintaining rapport. Is that correct?

Exactly, Jerome. It's all about showing guests that their comfort is a priority and that I'm here to make their stay as enjoyable as possible. This approach not only leads to happier guests but often results in better reviews and more repeat bookings.

Key Takeaways

1. Personalized Communication: Contact your guests as soon as they book. Use this opportunity to learn why they are visiting and personalize their experience. For instance, if they're interested in local culture, suggest some unique local attractions.

2. Importance of Feeling Valued: Make sure your guests feel valued and cared for right from the start. When you take a personal interest in their visit, they're more likely to overlook minor issues and feel positive about their stay, enhancing their overall experience.

3. Setting a Positive Tone: Early and personal interaction sets the right tone for the stay. Showing that you prioritize their comfort and satisfaction can lead to better reviews and encourage repeat bookings.

Action Item

- Develop a Welcome Protocol: If you're setting up a rental business, think about how you can make each guest feel welcomed and valued from the moment they book. Compile a list of information you'd like to gather from your guests, such as the purpose of their visit. Consider personalized touches you could add to their stay, like a custom guidebook or a welcome basket. This preparation helps you build strong rapport with guests and ensures a smooth hosting experience.

Secret 3: Ensuring Comfort and Safety

Norma, can you discuss how you ensure both comfort and safety in your listings?

Absolutely, Jerome. Ensuring that guests feel both comfortable and safe is crucial. Let's start with comfort. I don't skimp on furniture. For instance, I choose mattresses that provide the right balance of support. Not too soft, not too firm. It's important because, for example, I need a firm mattress to get up easily. But I also provide a variety of mattress types to cater to different preferences.

In my properties, especially in the primary bedrooms, I use high-quality Beauty Rest black mattresses and 700 to 800 thread count cotton sheets. These are not just comfortable but also durable and give a sense of luxury. Quality in these details shows guests that you care about their experience, which can reflect in their overall satisfaction and reviews.

And what about safety? How do you ensure guests feel secure?

For safety, I focus on a few key areas. First, I install sturdy locks and have a comprehensive security system, including cameras. I make sure to inform guests about the cameras for transparency and to reassure them of their safety. Another thing I use is keyless entry locks. I program the entry codes to be the last four digits of the guest's phone number. It's easy for them to remember, and it enhances security because it's unique to each guest.

That's really smart. Can you recap some specific steps our readers can take to enhance both comfort and safety in their rentals?

Certainly. For comfort, invest in upgraded furniture that not only looks good but is also durable and comfortable. Choose high-quality mattresses and offer a variety, if possible, to suit different preferences. For safety, enhance your outdoor lighting. It's important for visibility at night and adds to the property's security. Use reliable, easy-to-manage security features like keyless entry locks and ensure your property has a visible and effective security system.

Thanks, Norma. These practical tips not only enhance the guest experience but also build trust, which is crucial for repeat business.

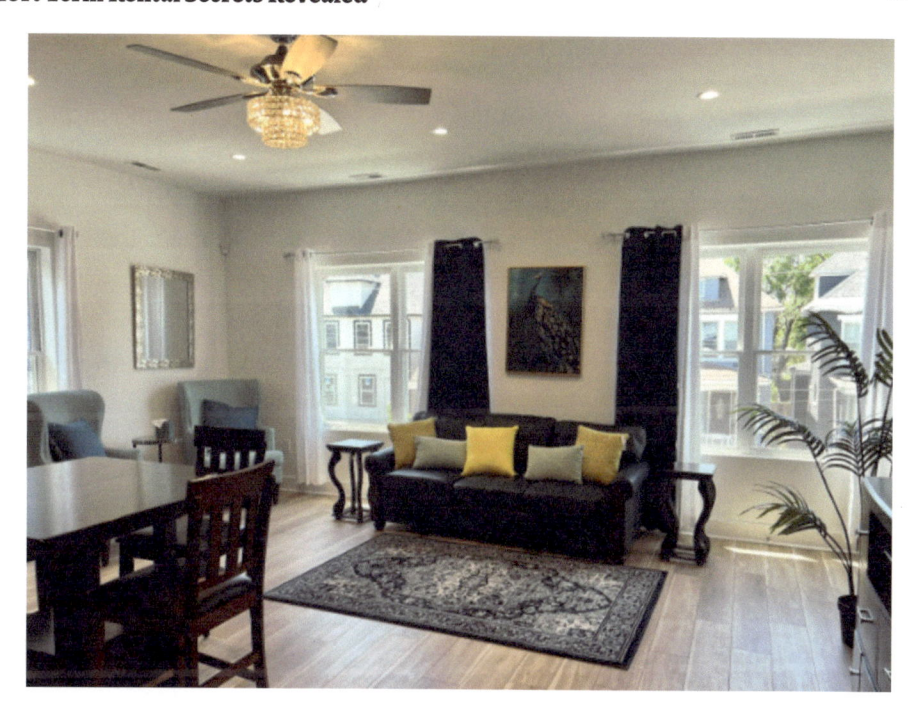

Key Takeaways

1. Investment in Quality: Norma stresses the importance of investing in high-quality furnishings, including mattresses, to ensure that guests have a comfortable stay. Stylish and functional furniture not only enhances the guest experience but also contributes to the overall aesthetic appeal of the listing.

2. Comprehensive Safety Measures: Implementing thorough safety measures such as effective lighting, sturdy locks, and security cameras is crucial. Norma ensures that these features are transparently communicated to guests, which helps in building trust and ensuring peace of mind during their stay.

3. Positive Impact on Reviews: The efforts put into ensuring comfort and safety are directly reflected in guest reviews. Satisfied guests often highlight these aspects, leading to better reviews and consequently, more bookings. This demonstrates the direct correlation between guest comfort, safety, and business success.

Action Item
- Evaluate Your Safety and Comfort Features: If you're planning to enter the short-term rental market, start by evaluating potential properties or your current property's furniture and safety features. Consider what upgrades might be necessary to meet the standards discussed. List enhancements like better mattresses, modern and functional furniture, and essential safety installations. Planning these upgrades in advance will help you set a budget and prioritize investments that will improve guest experiences and attract positive reviews.

Secret 4: Live in Your Listing

You mentioned living in your listing. Can you elaborate on that?

Absolutely, Jerome. Living in your listing is like a test drive for your rental. I recently did this with a new duplex I built. By staying there and going through my daily routines—getting up, showering, making breakfast—I could really understand the guest experience. This helps you spot any issues or discomforts that might not be obvious otherwise.

What kinds of things did you discover during your stay?

For one, the new bathtub had an anti-slip surface, which was great because it meant I didn't need a bathmat. But I also noticed it was a bit smaller than ideal, which could feel cramped for larger guests. In another bathroom, there's a large standalone shower, which would be more comfortable for someone who needs more space. Experiencing these details firsthand allows me to better advise future guests on which bathroom might suit them best based on their needs.

It sounds like living in the listing gave you valuable insights into how to improve guest comfort. How can hosts implement this practice effectively?

Hosts should stay in their rental as if they were the guests. Go through everything from using the kitchen appliances to sleeping in the beds. Note any small issues, whether it's something that needs fixing or just an improvement to make things more comfortable. This hands-on approach is the best way to ensure your property meets guest expectations.

Do you have any tips for what specifically to look for during such a stay?

Focus on the functionality and comfort of each area. Check things like the comfort of the sleeping arrangements, the ease of using the shower and kitchen facilities, and even how well the Wi-Fi works throughout the property. Also, consider the overall accessibility and convenience; how easy it is to move around the space, especially if you have guests with specific needs.

Norma, this approach really puts the host in the guest's shoes. What's the next step after identifying potential issues?

After identifying what needs to be improved, make those changes before your guests arrive. And remember, it's an ongoing process. Each stay in your property might reveal something new to enhance, which can continuously improve the guest experience.

Key Takeaways

1. Experience Your Property as a Guest: Spending time in your own rental property as if you were a guest is invaluable. It gives you firsthand insight into the guest experience, helping you see exactly what they see, from the small details to the overall atmosphere.

2. Identify Areas for Improvement: By staying in your listing, you can better identify any issues that could affect guest comfort, such as inadequate water pressure or uncomfortable furniture. Experiencing these issues yourself means you can fix them before they negatively impact your guests.

3. Ensure Guest Satisfaction: Addressing these issues not only enhances comfort but also ensures that guests have a pleasant stay, leading to better reviews and repeat bookings.

Action Item

- Perform a Stay Test in Your Rental: If you're setting up a new rental or want to improve your current one, take the time to stay there as a guest. Live in the space, use the amenities, and see what it's like to spend a day and night there. Make a list of any discomforts or potential improvements and prioritize fixing/upgrading them. This will help you provide a top-notch experience for your guests, leading to higher satisfaction and more successful bookings.

Secret 5: Cleanliness and Scent of Your Listing

How important are cleanliness and scent in your properties? Can you tell us about that, please?

Absolutely, Jerome. "Pristine Clean" is more than just a catchy phrase for my listings; it represents a commitment to the highest level of cleanliness and sanitization. Especially since the pandemic, guests are more conscious than ever about cleanliness. For instance, I have a property I call "Pristine Clean and Sanitized Business Paradise." It signals to guests that they can expect top-notch cleanliness, which has been a big draw.

How do you achieve this level of cleanliness, especially with back-to-back bookings?

It's all about not rushing the cleaning process, Jerome. I don't aim for 100% occupancy because it doesn't allow for thorough cleaning. Ideally, I prefer a few days between guests to perform a deep clean. This includes sanitizing every surface, from walls to baseboards, and even the ceiling fans. I also ensure that all fabrics, like curtains and furniture covers, are washed, and I replace rugs regularly.

And what about the scent of the listing? How important is that?

It's crucial, Jerome. The first thing guests notice when they enter a property is how it smells. If it's fresh and clean, that sets a positive tone for their stay. I avoid strong perfumes or scents that could trigger allergies. Instead, I opt for neutral, natural fragrances that are welcoming but not overwhelming. This approach helps ensure that all guests, regardless of their sensitivities, feel comfortable.

Can you share some specific strategies you use to maintain such high standards of cleanliness?

Of course. First, I ensure that the HVAC system is cleaned and the filters are changed regularly, which helps keep the air fresh and clean. For surfaces, I use a high-quality mop system that lets me quickly and effectively clean walls and floors. This system is easy to use and helps maintain a consistent standard of cleanliness. Lastly, I use luxury vinyl plank flooring in many of my properties because it's easier to keep clean and hygienic compared to carpet.

These details really show how much thought you put into every aspect of guest comfort. What would you say is the biggest takeaway for hosts about maintaining cleanliness?

The biggest takeaway would be that maintaining a high level of cleanliness and a pleasant scent isn't just about aesthetics; it's about guest safety and satisfaction. It requires planning and effort, but it pays off by enhancing guest experiences and encouraging repeat bookings. Always remember, the cleaner and fresher your property, the more appealing it will be to guests.

Key Takeaways

1. Essential Cleanliness: Keep your property spotlessly clean at all times. A clean environment is one of the first things guests notice, and it significantly impacts their overall impression and satisfaction.

2. Pleasant Scent: Ensure the scent of your property is fresh but not overwhelming. Using natural scents can greatly enhance the welcoming atmosphere of your rental.

3. Routine Maintenance: Regularly scheduled deep cleanings and maintenance, such as replacing air filters and checking the HVAC system, are crucial not only for maintaining cleanliness but also for ensuring the property smells fresh and has good air quality.

Action Item

- Implement a Cleaning and Maintenance Schedule: Set up a detailed cleaning checklist and maintenance schedule for your property. Include regular deep cleaning, frequent air filter changes, and HVAC system checks to keep your property in top condition. This will help ensure that your rental always meets high standards of cleanliness and comfort, making it more appealing to guests and potentially increasing your bookings.

Secret 6: Build a List

Why is building a list important with Short-Term Rentals? Can you share your perspective on that, please?

Sure, Jerome. Keeping a database is crucial for any business, especially in short-term rentals. I log each guest's name, phone number, and email address in a spreadsheet. This isn't just about having their information; it's about creating opportunities for repeat business. By maintaining this list, I ensure that I can contact past guests without relying solely on platforms like Airbnb or Vrbo, which often control communication.

How do you use this database to enhance guest experiences or encourage repeat visits?

I use it to stay connected. For instance, after guests check out, I send them a thank you message, and sometimes even special offers for their next stay. This personal touch makes guests feel valued and more likely to book again. Even though I haven't tapped into the full potential of the database for marketing campaigns yet, it's been instrumental in bringing guests back simply because they remember the personalized experience.

That sounds very effective. How do you collect these email addresses and phone numbers? Is there a specific approach you use, especially with platforms that don't readily provide this information?

With platforms like Vrbo, I get the guest's contact information directly after they book. However, Airbnb doesn't share guest emails, so I take a more personal approach. During our initial phone call, which I make to build rapport and confirm their booking details, I ask for their email to keep them updated. Most guests are happy to provide it, especially when they understand it's for enhanced communication and personalized offers.

And what about guests leaving items behind…You mentioned that helps you gather their addresses too?

Yes, that happens quite often—about 90% of the time, guests will forget something. I use this as another touchpoint to build trust and rapport. I contact them to arrange for their items to be sent back, which requires their address. It's another way to ensure they remember their stay positively and to maintain that connection.

It seems like maintaining your own guest list has multiple benefits, from marketing to improving guest relationships. Any final tips for hosts who want to start building their own list?

Start as soon as you can. Even if you're just beginning and have only a few guests, collect their information respectfully and use it to create a memorable experience. Remember, every detail you remember and every follow-up you make can turn a one-time guest into a returning visitor. And always ensure you handle their information with care and respect their privacy.

Key Takeaways

1. Keep Guests Coming Back: Regular emails keep your rental on guests' minds, increasing the chances they'll book with you again.

2. Make Guests Feel Special: An email list helps you create a sense of community. Guests who feel valued are more likely to return and spread the word.

3. Send Smarter Messages: Collecting emails lets you learn what your guests like, so you can send them tailored offers and updates that they're more likely to enjoy.

Action Item
- Start Collecting Emails Today: Make a plan to collect emails from your guests when they book and check out. You can add a simple sign-up form on your booking website or ask them during their stay. Explain that they'll get exclusive offers and fun updates from you, which makes joining the list more appealing. This step will help you stay connected and encourage guests to come back.

Secret 7: Set Up Your Listing Like a Business

Short Term Rental (STR) and Medium Term Rental (MTR) Businesses have tons of transactions. Keep up with them with this spreadsheet, it will make tax time a lot easier.

Start with this resource for keeping track of your expenses: **www.Etsy.com/shop/HappySpacesCo**

Norma, when you say, "set it up like a business," what exactly do you mean? How does setting up your rental like a business differ from not treating it like a business?

Jerome, treating your rental as a business means taking it seriously and professionally. It's not just about having a place to rent out; it's about ensuring that every aspect of the operation is optimized for success. For instance, a serious business owner would use an accounting program to keep track of finances. They'd also hire legal counsel to handle contracts to make sure everything is up to standard and legally sound.

So, you're saying that having professional systems in place is important. How about we address marketing? How important is that with your short-term rentals?

Marketing is absolutely critical, Jerome. You can have the best rental property out there, but if no one knows about it, you don't really have a business. Marketing helps bring guests to your door. It's about showcasing your property in such a way that it not only attracts guests but also entices them to book their stay with you.

It sounds like being proactive and involved is key. Could you expand on the importance of having a good product or service?

Definitely, Jerome. Having a solid product—meaning the rental itself—is fundamental. It needs to be clean, well-maintained, and appealing to guests. But beyond the physical aspects, the service you provide needs to be top-notch. This includes everything from customer service to the booking experience, and the stay itself. If the service or the product is lacking, it will reflect poorly on your business, and ultimately, you won't see the success you're aiming for.

Norma, for someone just starting out, what's the first step they should take to set up their rental as a business?

The first step is to recognize that you can't do everything alone. Start by identifying areas where you need help, like legal, accounting, or marketing. Hiring experts in these areas can make a huge difference. For legal and accounting, even basic professional assistance can help you set up the right structures and keep you compliant with regulations. For marketing, start simple with high-quality photos and descriptions for your listings, and consider investing in online marketing or social media to reach potential guests.

Norma, thanks for sharing your insights. It's clear that treating your rental like a business involves a mix of professionalism, quality service, and proactive marketing.

Key TakeAways

1. Professional Systems Are Crucial: Implementing professional accounting and legal systems helps ensure your rental operations are efficient, compliant, and protected against legal issues.

2. Marketing is Essential: To successfully run your rental as a business, effective marketing is key. It helps attract and retain guests by making your property known and appealing.

3. Quality of Product and Service: Maintaining a high-quality rental property and providing excellent service are fundamental. These aspects directly impact guest satisfaction and your business's reputation.

Action Item

- Evaluate Your Business Setup: Review your current setup for your rental property. Identify areas where you might need professional help, such as legal advice, accounting, or marketing. Consider hiring experts to ensure you're not only compliant with regulations but also effectively reaching potential guests. Start by enhancing your online presence with quality photographs and engaging descriptions of your property.

Secret 8: Independence from Third-Party Apps

Norma, we're now talking about an important topic—why it's not a good idea to rely only on online STR platforms to achieve short-term rental success. Can you explain why you think this independence is so important?

Absolutely, Jerome. What I mean is that relying solely on third-party rental platforms can be risky. They control the terms, and things can change overnight—whether it's a change in policies that affect how you operate, or even getting kicked off the platform without much notice. That's why having your own website is so important. It means you can still operate and communicate directly with your guests, regardless of what happens on those third-party platforms.

That makes sense. Why do you think many hosts fail to take this step?

Many hosts might feel overwhelmed by the idea of setting up a website or think it's not necessary as long as they are getting bookings through these platforms. But having your own site is about more than just bookings; it's about building a resilient business. No pun intended, but it's your virtual real estate. It's your online property, where you can showcase your rental exactly how you want and not be bound by the layout or rules of other platforms.

Can you give us some tips on what a good short-term rental website should include at a minimum?

Sure. At the very least, your website should include a bio that helps visitors understand who you are and why they should trust you with their stay. Include photos of your properties, descriptions, and features that highlight what makes your rentals special. Also, ensure you have contact information clearly visible so potential guests can reach you directly.

How has having your own short-term rental website impacted your business?

It's been transformative. It gives me full control over how I market my properties. I can highlight what truly sets my rentals apart without the constraints of a platform's format. Plus, it has helped build my brand's awareness and credibility, as well as attract repeat guests who appreciate the direct contact and personal touch.

What would you say to hosts who are hesitant about taking this step?

I would tell them that it's an investment in their business's future. In the digital age, your online presence is your business card. By having your own website, you're not just opening another booking channel; you're taking charge of your business's independence and security. Plus, with the right tools and support, setting up a website is easier than ever.

Thanks, Norma. It's clear that having your own website and being independent of third-party apps is crucial for the long-term success and stability of a rental business.

Key TakeAways

1. Reduce Reliance on External Platforms: It's risky to depend solely on sites like online STR platforms because they can have technical issues that might disrupt your ability to manage bookings and communicate with guests.

2. Control Your Business Operations: By managing your own bookings through a personal website, you have complete control over your rental business. This means direct access to guest information and more control during unexpected issues.

3. Save Money and Enhance Guest Relationships: Running your own booking site helps you save on fees charged by third-party platforms and allows for more personalized interactions with your guests, which can lead to repeat visits.

Action Item

- Create Your Own Booking Website: Start planning and developing a user-friendly website where guests can directly book their stays. Make sure the site is easy to use and provides all the necessary information a guest might need. This step will help you build a more stable and independent rental business.

Secret 9: The Importance of Building a Team

What is your perspective on building a team?

Well, that's a good question, Jerome. You have to have a team with you. You cannot do this by yourself. Although technology has really made it easier for people to run their own independent businesses like a sole proprietor, but I'm not a sole proprietor, I'm an LLC. I have a team that works with us, and I'm telling you, you can't do this by yourself. You need people who are experts in their areas to work with, like Jerome with the marketing. I have an attorney, I have an accountant, I have a bookkeeper, I have cleaners and maintenance people. I can't do all that, right?

Who do you think are the most important people to have on your team?

Well, it depends on the size of your business. I don't do all these things myself, but in the beginning – when I was growing my business – I was able to wear many hats. For example, when I had one unit, I could manage it and clean it myself. I was only listed on Airbnb at the time, and they have the legal stuff already in it. But when I grew and expanded, it became important for me to have an attorney to draw documents that I needed because you need agreements between the cleaning staff. And I would say the cleaners are the most important aspect when you're running more than one listing. You have to be fair, pay them a fair wage, and be concerned about them because they can make or break your business. As I indicated, my listing is called "Pristine Clean and Sanitized." I can't clean and sanitize all these units that I manage, so my cleaning staff and the contractors that I work with, I pay them fairly. I make sure that I have several cleaning teams that I can access simply because they have lives too, and you don't want to put the pressure on them that they have to always be there. They can take time for their kids or their health or whatever it is that they need to do. Have multiple cleaning teams takes the pressure off – you and them. And of course, you have to balance that because you want them to all have consistent work, but you also want to make sure that if they can't make it, you don't make them feel bad. Remember, the same way you have a life outside of your short-term rental business, so do the members of your team.

Okay, so here's how I would recap what you have said thus far:

1. The Proper Mindset: Number one, you've got to be in the right mindset, you've got to have the right training, and you've got to be committed to this process. In order to build a team, we have to be successful and strong ourselves.

2. A Legal Professional/Attorney: When you're growing and you're getting bigger, you need an attorney.

3. A Cleaning Team: You need a cleaning team that can help keep your short-term rental in order and they will help things run smoothly.

4. A Mentor/Coach: I think you need a mentor or a coach, and I think people forget about that as being part of their team.

What would you say about the last point regarding a mentor or coach?

Well, you're absolutely right, Jermone, you do need a mentor or coach, and I have mentored many people. When I first got into the short-term rental business, I don't think I had a mentor because it was so new. I had to figure it out on my own. I was introduced to short-term rentals through my children because they used to travel, or they still travel a lot, and they would tell me that they're staying at an Airbnb, and I was like, what the heck is that? It's not even a word, "Air B and B," you know, it needs another vowel or two. But anyway, they explained what it meant, air mattress, bread and breakfast. I stayed in a few of them with my kids. I never met any of the owners, though. I never met any of the owners, so I had to just figure it out on my own. But since, you know, I've been in contact with so many other hosts and real estate investors, I have mentored lots of people.

Key Takeaways

1. Teamwork Makes the Dream Work: Managing a rental property involves a lot of different tasks. As your business grows, you'll need help to handle everything from cleaning to maintenance. This helps you keep up with the demands of running a successful rental.

2. Start with Cleaners: A clean rental is crucial for good guest reviews and repeat business. Having reliable cleaners is the first step to ensuring your property is always guest-ready.

3. Expand Your Team as Needed: As your rental business grows, the need for additional support like maintenance personnel, legal advisors, and marketing experts will increase. Building a team gradually lets you maintain quality and manage tasks more efficiently.

Action Item

- Evaluate Your Current Needs: Take a moment to think about your rental business. Are you overwhelmed by certain tasks? Could hiring a cleaner, handyperson, or marketing help free up your time and improve your service? Make a list of roles that could help you manage your rental more effectively and consider hiring for these positions to better support your business's growth.

Secret 10: Conclusion

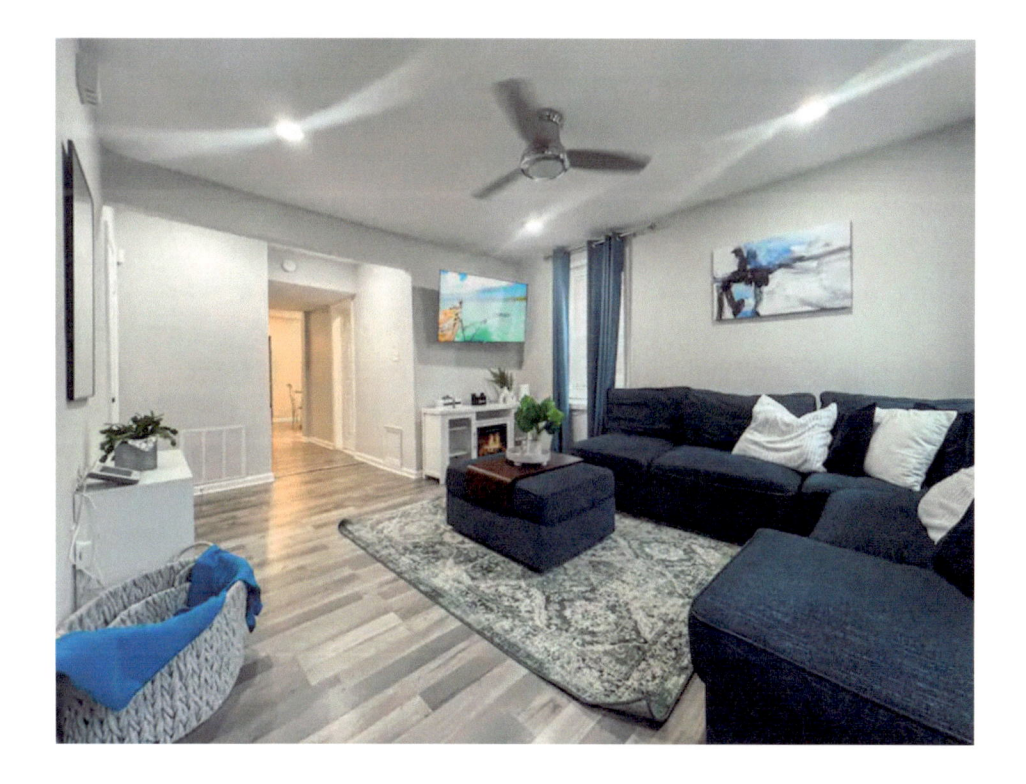

Norma, you offer services regarding short-term rentals. Can you tell us how to get in touch with you if we are interested in your services?

Absolutely. You can get in touch with me by going to HappySpacesLLC.com. My contact information is on that website, and they'll get access to both my services and the mentorship. They can contact me for mentorship or if they have a property and want to create a listing for, make a listing on Airbnb, etc., I can assist them with that. I just did that this weekend with a young man who bought a property, and I actually have one of his properties now, but he brought another property, and he wanted to make sure that it was set up in a way that it would be efficiently run if we do a short-term rental with it. I told him what he needed to do. I actually worked with another young man, and we looked at several properties. It took him a year to find the perfect property, so you have to have patience as well. I do mentor, and I know that you have to have the right situation. In other words, you have to go into the property right, so that the expenses are not going to be so high that you don't make enough money, but that's another story.

Norma, thank you so much. What would you say to anybody that's trying to have success in short-term rentals?

Well, actually, there are some other things that we could have talked about, but if I wanted to summarize this conversation, I would say that I think in order to be successful with your short-term rental business, understand that it's a hospitality business, and things have to be addressed immediately. If anything goes wrong, you don't have a lot of time to redeem yourself. Guests have to feel like you care about them. That's the whole thing about building a rapport with people is that you care, and you're not just in this for the financial gain. I think that's the most important thing that people need to feel. They need to feel like you care about them.

Alright, Norma, thank you so much.

You are so welcome.

Key Takeaways

1. Hospitality Over Business: Success in short-term rentals isn't just about making money; it's about caring genuinely for your guests and responding promptly to their needs.

2. Quick Response is Crucial: When issues arise, acting fast to solve them shows your guests that you value their comfort and experience, reinforcing their trust in your service.

3. Build Lasting Rapport: Consistently showing that you care about your guests' experiences can lead to repeat bookings, positive reviews, and ultimately, a successful rental business.

Action Item

- Implement a Guest Feedback System: Set up a simple way for guests to provide feedback on their stay. This could be through a follow-up email or a physical feedback form in the rental. Use this feedback to identify areas for improvement and show guests that their opinions are valued and taken seriously. This step will help you enhance your service and demonstrate your commitment to guest satisfaction.

What To Do Next

Congratulations on finishing Short-Term Rental Secrets! You're now equipped and empowered with Norma Richards' valuable insights and practical advice on thriving in the short-term rental market. So, what's next? Whether you prefer to take on tasks yourself, need a little guidance, or want someone to handle things for you, we've got options to help you move forward.

DIY: Do It Yourself with Norma's Course

If you're the hands-on type and like to manage things yourself, consider diving deeper with a comprehensive course. Norma has developed an online course that breaks down everything from property selection to guest management in detailed, step-by-step lessons. This self-paced course is perfect if you want to strengthen your knowledge base and apply what you've learned at your own speed. You'll get access to exclusive content that builds on the book, including templates and checklists to streamline your operations.

DWY: Do It With Help Using Coaching/Consultation Services

Sometimes, a little personalized guidance can make all the difference. If you feel you would benefit from some direct support, Norma offers coaching and consultation services. This is a great way to get specific advice tailored to your unique situation. Whether you're encountering challenges or just want to ensure you're on the right track, scheduling a session with Norma can provide you with the expertise and confidence to excel. Coaching sessions are available on an hourly basis, or you can opt for a package deal depending on your needs.

DFY: Done For You by Hiring Norma

If you're busy or prefer not to manage the day-to-day operations of your rental, Norma's full-service management might be the perfect solution. With the "Done For You" option, Norma and her team take over the management of your property. From marketing your rental to handling guest communications and ensuring your property is impeccably maintained, they'll take care of everything. This option is ideal if you want to enjoy the benefits of investment in real estate without the daily responsibilities.

How to Proceed

Explore the Course: Visit HappySpacesLLC.com/course to learn more about the course and enroll. Start whenever you're ready and go at your own pace.

Book a Consultation: If you're interested in personalized coaching, check out the coaching section on our website to book your first session.

Inquire About Management Services: For full management services, contact Norma directly via email at HappeeSpaces@gmail.com to discuss your needs and how we can help manage your rental property efficiently.

Action Item

- You've already taken a great step by educating yourself with this book. Now, choose the path that best suits your goals and resources, and take your short-term rental business to new heights. Norma and her team are here to help you succeed every step of the way!

About The Author: Norma Richards

What NormaRichards.com has accomplished in real estate in a few short years was driven by 3 factors:
1. An itty bitty social security check
2. An itty bitty retirement account
3. Coupled with a very high standard of living and expenses.

Even more important, she wanted to teach her children how to build wealth. So she set out to become a house flipper, wholesaler, short term rental host, and now, a real estate developer success story in five short years, dramatically increasing her family's net worth.

Now, this mom is on a mission to help others do the same. Her goal is to turn ``I cannot afford real estate" into, you can't afford not to do real estate. There are so many opportunities: note buying, wholesaling, flipping, etc. she encourages everyone to find their niche and step out of the box, stop being afraid, educate yourself and take the leap.

A microbiologist and science teacher by trade, Norma set out to prove it can be done. She did her homework and discovered there really is a science to acquiring real estate by reading and studying real estate investor practices.

A native of Flint, Michigan, Norma is a successful entrepreneur and certified science teacher in the state of Ohio. She earned a Bachelors of Science in Microbiology from Howard University in Washington D.C., and has called Columbus, Ohio home for over 30 years.

Norma and her husband now spend their time traveling the country, entertaining friends and relishing quiet evenings enjoying HGTV and their favorite Turner Classic Movies—life is good.

She is happy to share with you points about her real estate journey and business…And even more excited to introduce the New Facebook live venture with a fellow real estate investor, Jerome Lewis, "The Short Term Rental News Network" where she leads discussions related to the ever changing short term rental business. And talk about her upcoming book, Short Term Rental Secrets Revealed .

Real Estate Bio

Norma Richards joined The Community of Real Estate Entrepreneurs (COREE) when it was called the Central Ohio Real Estate Entrepreneurs (COREE). Since being introduced to COREE by member, Tancy Mason-Philips, she has found a new love in Real Estate. Hailing from the Great City of Columbus, Ohio, Norma has been excited about every aspect of Real Estate Investing. She has explored and executed wholesaling, flipping, Short Term Rentals, Mid Term Rental and even Real Estate development. She finally decided she enjoyed making travelers happy, and founded the company Happy Spaces LLC. This company operates over twenty short term and medium term rentals in Ohio, Michigan, California and Washington, DC. In addition, the real estate development company J and N properties focuses on land acquisitions and the erection of multi family dwellings.

How long have you been in real estate?

I have been exposed to the real estate business since I was a child. My grandmother and my dad owned and managed multi family properties in Michigan when I was growing up. I have five brothers, and I was the only girl. My brothers were taught how to fix almost anything in a house and even build a house. Since I was the only girl, my mom and I were relegated to cleaning the properties, cooking and getting our hair done. So I didn't really learn a lot about how to maintain the properties, but I was exposed from a young age thanks to my dad and grandmother.

Fast forward to modern times, I dabbled in real estate about 30 years ago. My husband and I purchased a single-family home, which we rented. We actually paid too much for the property to be a rental. We really didn't know what we were doing. We had all kinds of issues with the tenants i.e. not paying the rent, letting their pets destroy the property, putting sugar down in the air ducts etc. So we sold the house and got out of real estate.

Fast forward to contemporary times. Just like the Internet has even the playing field for many other businesses, it has done the same thing for real estate. I have been in the short term rental (STR) business since 2017. But the real catalyst for me was My kids. They are all engineers and are a part of the National Society of Black Engineers (NSBE) an organization that helps college students obtain internships in engineering. In 2017 I started renting rooms in my primary residence to college students. Since then I have acquired more properties in Michigan, Ohio and Washington DC as short term rentals thanks to the internet.

What is your real job or was your Last Real Job?

I am actually a microbiologist. I've worked as a lab technician, health inspector and teacher. I really enjoyed being an educator, teaching biological science for many years.

However, in addition, I have been a serial entrepreneur all my life too. I was really born to be in business. I owned a retail women's apparel store for 20 years. I've had several Internet businesses. But most recently, before I really got into real estate, I authored the book

Free Ride to College: A Guide to Grooming Your Kids For a Full Academic Scholarship aka FreeRidetoCollege.com I wrote the book because, despite the fact that my kids were labeled Attention Deficit Hyperactivity Disorder (ADHD), special education, and the youngest was almost legally blind, they all earned full academic scholarships to college and they are all engineers now.

Consequently, I saved close to a half a million dollars in college expenses. So, before I got back into real estate, I was traveling the country doing college readiness and scholarship expos.

If members saw you at a meeting, what could you talk to them about? (real estate or non-real estate related), :

I would talk about the fact that previously, I didn't understand at first how my experience helping families send their kids to college for free was related to real estate. Now that my kids are buying real estate, I see there is a clear connection between going to college for free versus having to take out student loans to pay for college. The bottom line is, it's much easier to qualify for a mortgage without huge amounts of student loan debt.

What first got you interested in real estate investing?

Recently, I honestly think watching HGTV, along with my kids introducing me to Airbnb really drove me back into real estate. I can't watch sports all day like my son, brothers, dad and husband, nor do I like horrible movies, murder mysteries etc. I like to read and watch non-fiction books and programs. So besides the history channel, HGTV is one of my favorite networks. That network definitely inspired me to take it further and do my own real estate business. Furthermore, my kids kept telling me about Airbnb. At first I just could not wrap my head around it. Air B and What?

There are not enough vowels in the word, so it did not make sense to me. Then I traveled with my daughter and my son and we stayed at Airbnbs. They were pleasant experiences and I learned that I could make money renting out my properties.

What was your first deal, or your first set of deals, like? What were your challenges, what did you learn, how did it/they turn out?

My first renovation was not really a deal; I renovated my dad's house. Next I renovated my primary residence and then I thought I could really be a rehabber. Of course I had been looking at all the HGTV shows and admiring their results. At this point, I wanted to get into real estate so badly, I was willing to buy this half burned down house to renovate because it was cheap. I know now, it is not about cheap, it is about return on investment. That was a crazy thought but it shows how anxious I was.

But my first real renovation was a house I bought from a private home owner. I did not even close at a title company, which I don't recommend! I did check with the Franklin County Recorder's office though to find out about the liens and I made the checks out to the lien holders. That was supposed to be a cosmetic renovation. I was told it would take about five thousand dollars to fix. Well that is not what happened, I spent close to 70 thousand dollars to fix the property. The lesson I learned, there really is no such thing as a cosmetic flip!

What are your big goals for the year?

My goals for this year include: getting my kids into their first investment property, completing my first project as a real estate developer, and finally, purchasing a multi family building along with my children and siblings. My daughter and I have already tackled the challenging and expensive Washington, DC market. Next I'm going out west to help my son in the outrageously expensive San Diego, California market. Although I have purchased two newly built family homes from other developers, it is quite a different experience now that I am the developer. I'm learning a lot building my first duplex. I love a challenge and we are certainly up to it.

What's your favorite type of deal right now?

Everything has pros and cons! It just depends on my tolerance level at the time. I do love to renovate and come with a transformed property, it's fun, but risky and expensive. I just finished a renovation for a colleague. I also like wholesale because it is a little quicker and I don't need money.

Now that I am a developer it has pros and cons too.

If you could give your younger self some real estate advice, what would it be?

I would say make purchasing real estate a priority instead of cars and clothes. After I graduated from Howard University in Washington, DC. I wanted to buy a building there. So, I asked my dad to send me a few thousand dollars to buy a building. Of course he was very impressed and sent the money. But, instead of buying the property, I bought a brand new Chevrolet Monte Carlo, silver with burgundy velvet seats, and a Tee top, I was riding pretty. I really regret that now, I should have invested the money in real estate and studied real estate when I was younger. If I had bought property investment years ago in DC. it would be worth a lot of money now. That's why I'm making it my business, to make sure my kids buy investment property.

If you could give other members just one piece of advice, what would it be?

Just say encouraging words to another investor that is sometimes all people need.

What do you love about real estate?

I love doing real estate because it makes people happy to have a clean, comfortable and inspirational space to live in. Life is short and people need happy spaces to dwell in while they're here. That is the reason I called my business Happy SpacesLLC, I really do want people to feel happy in my spaces.

About Happy Spaces LLC

Happy Spaces, LLC has been a short-term rental host for over six years and has been investing in real estate for over 20 years. Our team manages over 22 Five-star Medium and short-term rentals nationwide and we pride ourselves on superior customer service and clean comfortable spaces.

Real estate has been in Norma Richards's family for two generations. She first learned real estate watching her father manage rental properties in Flint, Michigan. Her problem-solving skills have been fine-tuned during her many years providing solutions to clients and guests while working in the short-term rental industry. She is an author and proud graduate of Howard University having majored in Microbiology. Before getting into real estate full-time, Norma owned her own women's boutique in Columbus, Ohio and her eye for design and style translates into her creativity in interior design.

Happy Spaces, LLC's mission and vision are tucked right into the name of the company. Their mission is to create clean, safe spaces that guests can enjoy, and a superior customer service experience for both hosts and guests alike.

Want Help Creating Setting Up Your Short-Term Rental?

Are you ready to take all the Secrets you learned in this book and put them to work?

Then Norma wants to help you!

Email: **HappeeSpaces@gmail.com** to see if Norma can help you:

Just email HappeeSpaces@gmail.com with the subject line "STR Secrets"

Made in the USA
Columbia, SC
14 November 2024